SEASONS

A Christian Love Story

Rick Miller

TABLE OF CONTENTS

*"Beloved, let us love one another because
love is from God,
And everyone who loves is begotten
of God and knows God."
1st John 4:7*

CHAPTER ONE

─────────────〜─────────────

"When one finds a worthy wife,
her value is far beyond pearls."
Proverbs 31:10

The telecast streamed from the Oval Office in the White House. It was 11 January 1989. President Ronald Reagan was nearing the end of His Farewell Address to the nation. It was a bittersweet moment. He was a good man and he had done well. I was grateful for what he had done for us. I pondered the question he had asked; how does America stand "this winter night?" Offering his own answer, Mr. Reagan said, "After 200 years, two centuries, she still stands strong and true on the granite ridge, and her glow has held steady no matter what storm."

Indeed, America has weathered many storms. Some have really been bad. Caught up in the moment I reflected on how God-fearing, optimistic and purpose driven leaders like Mr. Reagan provide the leadership vital for us to weather the storms we encounter. The thought came to mind, in the great storms of both a personal and professional nature that he had faced, President Reagan had been buoyed by his beloved wife, Nancy. Their enduring love affair, their closeness, their fierce protection of and dependency on one another was a love story for the ages. The sadness I felt about seeing the president go stirred deeper emotions in me from the passing of my wife over a decade ago. In some ways I feel as though she is still with me. Named for her father's home town and the flowers it was famous for, my wife Tyler Rose was to me what Nancy Reagan was to her husband.

I looked to the mantle above the fireplace. I focused my attention on the small Alamo snow globe. Tyler had given it to me on our tenth wedding anniversary. Basking in the warmth of remembrance, I imagined her sweet voice urging me to "remember the Alamo."

Tyler and I first met, long ago on May 29th, Memorial Day, 1967. Remembering the thrill and sense of wonder I felt still enthralls me. Tyler had been with a group of three or four other young ladies at the Alamo. As she backed away from an exhibit inside the Chapel, she ran into me and stepped on my foot. Had I not caught her at her elbows and stopped her backward momentum, we both would have fallen.

As she turned around, I was awe-struck by the petite, perky little red head, a breath-taking enchantress with a killer smile. Tyler looked up at me with her captivating hazel eyes that shined like polished gemstones. She smelled like vanilla spice. In a voice slightly above a whisper, in deference to the Shrine of Liberty we were in, she apologized profusely. "Oh my gosh, oh my gosh. I am so sorry. I am so sorry." Tyler's sweet heavily accented Texas drawl made me swoon. She wore white turquoise studded western boots, a pretty beige cotton dress hemmed well above her knees and she had a gorgeous bronze, Texas tan. I blushed. Why is it I wondered that a man's knees buckle and his pulse races when he comes face to face with a beautifully proportioned young lady?

That had been the beginning of what would be a whirlwind romance that ended in marriage and ten blessed years of blissful union. Tyler had been an answer to prayer. She had been the most amazing find of my life. God is love and those who abide in love abide in God and He in them. In the abiding love Tyler and I shared, a love "brighter than the brightest of flames and stronger than death," we experienced God and enjoyed a foretaste of Heaven.

I thought again about President Reagan's question and how it applied to my own life. Sitting on the love seat Tyler had insisted we buy, still nestled up close to the fireplace where she liked it, I clung to the neatly folded olive drab army blanket she liked to snuggle up in. I looked into the reddish-orange glow of the fireplace. The logs hissed, crackled and popped, occasionally shooting sparks toward the screen. In the air there was the comforting aroma of the vanilla spice candle, brewing coffee and burning fire-wood. I felt blessed and grateful. God had given me the opportunity to live life to the fullest. He had given me Tyler to make that so.

3

For years I couldn't bring myself to do anything with Tyler's personal things. Finally, I decided it was time to let some things go. Just today, our best friends and next-door neighbors, Carmen and Mike Reid came over to take care of everything. They were a God-send. Mike got me out of the house. We went ice fishing while Carmen gathered a lot of nice things together and took them over to the Salvation Army. She only left the keepsakes I treasured most, Tyler's favorite pink dress, her old college sweater and the pair of jeans she thought too tight. I thought just right.

As was my habit at day's end, I turned to Scripture. I opened the Holy Bible to Ecclesiastes. The lesson the Good Lord reminded me of that winter night, aside from Him and the good people and goodness He brings into our lives, "all is vanity and a chase after wind." I bowed my head and dropped to my knees. I thanked God for Tyler. I thanked Him for the good people and goodness He had brought into my life. I thanked Him for giving me the grace to take things in stride and accept the humbling reality that there is a season and time for every purpose under Heaven.

CHAPTER TWO

"a time for love . . ."
Ecclesiastes 3: 8

T hanks to my parents I had been brought up with a steady dose of Church going and Scripture reading. So, growing up I had a Biblical notion of romance that had never panned out for me. In my heart I still believed there were some marriages made in Heaven and I looked to the examples cited in Scripture, Jacob and Rachel, Tobias and Sarah, Ruth and Boaz, Esther and King Xerxes, the lovers in the Song of Solomon, and of course, Joseph and Mary.

History is fickle in that both good times and bad times can overlap. There can be both the best of times and worst of times, at the same time. That is how it was when Tyler and I were blessed to meet, fall in love and start our journey of life together.

Back in the late spring of 1967 I lived and worked in Colorado Springs, Colorado, a growing community at the foot of Pikes Peak and the Rocky Mountains. I was an inactive Marine Reservist, junior high school history teacher and freelance journalist. It was a tumultuous time for America.

There were many Americans who thought we were in an irreversible state of decline that had begun with the assassination of President John Kennedy. Some argued our military involvement in South Vietnam was being mismanaged. Many others argued we shouldn't be there in the first place. Violent anti-war protests dotted the nation. The peaceful work to secure equal rights for minorities had taken a violent turn and there had been terrible race riots in places like Los Angeles, Atlanta and Chicago. More and more people discarded traditional values. There was increasing glorification of premarital sex and prevalent use of illegal drugs. All in all, there was grave loss of respect for institutions like the Church and the military. President Kennedy had set America on the path to beat the Russians to the moon but the recent loss of the three brave Apollo 1 Astronauts in the tragic accident at Cape Canaveral fueled feelings our country was headed downhill.

It was in such a setting that I decided to take the summer break from teaching to go on an assignment for a Christian news magazine. "The Christian Focus" had hired me to do a feature on the Christian view of military service. All the ducks had been lined up. All the necessary coordination had been done for us to spend time with a reserve Marine Corps Rifle Company in Austin, Texas and then tour Marine Corps Recruit Depot in San Diego, California. Both of which I was intimately familiar with.

My itinerary called for me to meet up with an old friend of mine, photojournalist "Hitch" Hitchcock in San Antonio, on Sunday the 28th of May. We planned to spend Memorial Day doing a little sight-seeing. We had to be in Austin early Tuesday afternoon to begin our visit with Company B, 1st Battalion, 23rd Marine Regiment, 4th Marine Division.

Hitch was a former Marine too. We had served together and later teamed up in civilian life to work on articles for a Civil War magazine that covered the Battles of Fredericksburg and Gettysburg. Hitch was a good Christian and a top notch professional and cheerful guy to be around.

Not an hour after we left the Alamo, Hitch and I were eating lunch at a little Mexican café on the bank of the River Walk. It was a nice little place but the tables were too crowded together and there was little room to squeeze between them. Just as I had put a glass of ice tea to my mouth, I was bumped from behind and spilled the tea all over the table. As I stood up and turned around, I noted the scent of vanilla spice and was pleasantly surprised to once again encounter the very same clumsy, but stunningly beautiful southern belle that had tripped over me in the Alamo. Again, in an accent that made my heart melt, she said, "Mister, I am again so very sorry, truly I am. This just isn't my day. Please forgive me." She then seemed to be at a loss as to how to address me, "Mister?"

I seized upon the opportunity. I told her my name was Josh, Joshua Taylor. In turn she told me her name was Tyler Rose Devine. I grinned and knew she had probably read my mind. I was certain she had heard the particular response I was thinking a thousand times. Even though I was thinking it, I kept the thought to myself, "divine you certainly are."

Tyler then said something along the lines that it was nice to meet me. I returned the sentiment. As she walked away, I heard Hitch trying to get my attention, "psst." I turned to him and with his right hand he pointed down at his left, laughing under his breath he whispered, "she doesn't have a ring."

"Too young," I whispered back but caught myself trying not to stare as she seemed to float away, an ethereal creature if ever there was one. Tyler then bumped into another table before reaching her companions seated in the corner.

*   *   *

Our hotel was near the Alamo and we decided to make a leisurely morning of it before driving the 80 miles to Austin for our two o'clock appointment. Before leaving for Camp Mabry, I decided to buy a few post cards at the nearby Kress Five and Dime. As Hitch and I perused the souvenir rack, I felt a sharp punch to my side. I looked at Hitch and he pointed at the food counter in the back of the store. "Do you see what I see?" he asked. There, behind the counter was the pretty young lady that twice ran into me the day before. She was wearing a pretty pink uniform. The large pink ribbon she wore complimented her ravishing red hair. "If it were me," said Hitch, "I'd at least go say 'Hi.'" "I'm too old for her," said I. "You're a chicken," said he.

After debating with myself I decided to throw caution to the wind.

I went over to the food counter and slid slowly onto a stool. I didn't want to be too obvious. I audibly cleared my throat. Again, I noted the pleasing fragrance of vanilla spice as Tyler walked over to me with a coffee pot. When our eyes met, I was delighted she recognized me. She smiled, "You're safe this time," she said, "There's a counter between us."

One cup of coffee turned into two. The minutes passed into an hour and a half. I could have sat there all day listening to her talk. Her Texas accent, what some call a southern accent with a twist, was hypnotic. Tyler really seemed to be interested in me and she must have been able to tell the feeling was mutual. Thank God she wasn't very busy. The breakfast rush was over and only one other customer was at the counter and he was busy with his scrambled eggs and newspaper. We really had a wonderful, wonderful conversation. My friend Hitch may have been really bored waiting for me but those were among the most pleasant 90 minutes in my life.

As I said, named for Tyler, Texas and the roses it is famous for, Tyler was from Yoakum, Texas. She was a Christian, Roman Catholic no less and a student up the road at Southwest Texas State College in San Marcos. She had just graduated summa cum laude with her Bachelor's Degree and had a few more classes to take over the summer to finish her teaching certification. She hoped to get a teaching job in, I was floored, Colorado Springs because she wanted to be near her brother, Senior Airman Travis Lee Devine, USAF who was headed up to the Springs.

Tyler and her brother were very close. They were fraternal twins born just minutes apart on Valentine's Day, February 14, 1946. After being orphaned at an early age, they had been raised by their aunt, Ruth Prouser. Travis saw himself as the "older" brother because he had been born twenty minutes before his sister. He had an obsession for taking care of his "younger sister" and had made a solemn promise to their aunt to keep an eye on her "little rose." Tyler and Travis lived together in an apartment near Randolph Air Force Base. At the time he was a crew chief on Cessna T-37 "Tweet" trainers but had been accepted for attendance at the United States Air Force Academy Preparatory School, in Colorado Springs.

Initially I was bothered by the obvious age thing. Tyler was 21. I had just turned 28 but we did share a lot of things in common. We were both practicing Christians. Both of us were in education. We both loved country music. Patsy Cline and newcomer Tammy Wynette were our favorites. We both liked baseball and our favorite team was the Houston Astros, not necessarily a perennial power house but a local favorite. It also turned out that her aunt subscribed to the magazine I was working for.

Tyler seemed to especially perk up when I told her I was from Colorado Springs and would be in Texas for a couple of weeks. She seemed to be really taken that I had been a Marine infantryman. She was noticeably proud when she spoke of Her father, a Marine too. He had fought with the 1st Marine Division at Guadalcanal in World War Two and later paid the ultimate sacrifice at the Chosin Reservoir in the Korean War. Tyler made a point of leaning over the counter to show me her father's Marine Corps "Eagle, Globe and Anchor" tie clasp she had made into a pendant for her neckless.

Her mother had passed away from lymphatic cancer when she was only in her 30s and Tyler was obsessed with making her parents proud of her. "I want the Good Lord to be proud of me too," she had added.

Tyler was a hardworking young lady. When classes were in session, she had afternoon classes every day of the week except Friday. On Friday she helped out as student teacher at Crocket Elementary School. Weekends Tyler worked at the Randolph Base Exchange. In what spare time she had, she was involved with the Big Brother/ Big Sister program. Yes, she said, she had a couple of boy-friends but nothing serious. Mostly, when she could, she bummed around with her girl-friends. They liked to sun bathe and bowl.

Feeling another punch to the side, Hitch had to remind me that we needed to get on the road. It was heart wrenching to part but through the grace of God I mustered the courage to face rejection and told Tyler I'd like to see her again. I can't describe the joy I felt when she responded, "I'd like to see you again too." It took my breath away when Tyler wrote her phone number on a napkin, saying with a smile, "you can give me a call tonight, if you'd like." That napkin is still in an old photo album I have on the coffee table.

When we got outside, I did something spontaneous which was out of character for me. I saw a vendor on the other side of the street selling flowers. I darted out into the busy city traffic and dodged four lanes of buses and cars. Tyler smiled when I returned and handed her a single yellow rose.

Off and on during our trip to Austin, Hitch poked fun at me by singing "The Yellow Rose of Texas." The song did allude to an exciting possibility. Just maybe there was some truth in the words of the song. In the silence of my heart I sang along too.

> "There's a yellow rose in Texas,
> I'm going down to see . . .
> she's the sweetest little rose
> that I have ever knew.
> Her eyes are bright as diamonds,
> they sparkle like the dew.
> You may talk about your dearest Mae
> and sing of Rosa Lee
> but the Yellow Rose of Texas
> beats all the girls I've ever seen."

It took Hitch and I about an hour and forty-five minutes to drive to the Marine Corps Reserve Center at Camp Mabry in Austin. Our meeting with the Company Commander turned out to be a real eye opener. In addition to Major Jack Stein, his second in command, Captain Tony Mena, in attendance were Federal Bureau of Investigation Special Agent Stew Livingston and an old friend from the Texas Department of Public Safety, Bubba Reilly. Bubba was the chief of the DPS Tactical Operations Branch of the Texas Rangers.

Our curiosity was really peaked as Hitch and I were introduced to each individual. When we got around to Bubba, I asked, "What in the heck did we do to get the FBI and Texas Rangers after us?" He just grinned.

After we all sat down at the conference table, Major Stein, who was seated in the head chair, looked around at everyone and was silent for a very long time.

"Gentlemen," he finally started talking, "we have a situation here." He looked intently at Hitch and I. "We had initially thought it best to cancel the setup we had with you but my superiors and the folks here thought it might be an asset to have what's fixing to take place reported on by a sympathetic source. And," the major stopped in midsentence and made the sternest expression. He barked, "and you two, 1st Lieutenant Taylor and Staff Sergeant Hitchcock had better give us the sympathetic coverage we're expecting." Now years later, it still amuses me to recall how Hitch and I jumped to attention in our chairs and shouted, "Aye, Aye Sir!"

Turned out, back on the east coast, an informant for the FBI had identified a former Marine reservist, Corporal Gerald Spence as a leader of a communist activist cell comprised of four other bad-guys. They were headed to Texas to cause mischief with an audacious scheme to procure weapons for their organization. Former member of Company B that he was, Spence was familiar with the unit deployment procedures. He knew that the 130

Marines would be travelling with 130 or more M-16 rifles and M-60 machine guns but only the commander and first sergeant would have loaded weapons. The Company B convoy always stopped at the Roadside Park between San Antonio and San Marcos so the troops could stretch their legs and use the facilities. The plan of the insurgents was simple enough. They would attack the trucks when they parked and take out the major and first shirt and easily make off with a boat load of lethal weapons.

Normally drills were conducted Friday through Sunday but because of scheduling conflicts with Army National Guard units, the June drill had to be done during the week, i.e. the last day of May and first two days of June. The east coast informant had told the FBI that after gathering the publicly available information, the communist sympathizers planned to strike Friday afternoon, June 2nd when Company B made its return trip home.

Hitch and I, as planned, were to accompany the unit to Camp Bullis Army National Guard Training Center. At drills end, the 130 reservists were not to return in the truck convoy. They'd be bused back to Austin later in the day. We'd be with the convoy as the "sympathetic" reporters.

Because the Posse Comitatus Act prohibits federal military forces from enforcing civil law, well-armed and well-trained law enforcement personnel would be in the trucks instead. The Texas Ranger Special Weapons and Tactics personnel, backed up by the FBI were sure to catch the bad guys flat footed. Hitch and I would be spectators with the Navy corpsman in the military ambulance at the tail end of the convoy.

I asked Ranger Reilly why they just didn't arrest Spence and his crew before the attack. "Surely," I said, "there must be some legal grounds to do that."

The big problem, Bubba answered, was that law enforcement did not have the identities of all the other bandits. The best way to handle the situation was to get them all in one fell swoop when they were all together.

Major Stein swore us to secrecy, then told us to stop by supply for an issue of gear, boots and utilities. It felt good to be in "mean green" again. We zipped back to the hotel for an early dinner and early turn in. Our morning would start in the wee dark hours. Needless to say, regardless of what happened, one thing was for certain. From that point on, the reservists would have law enforcement escort and travel with loaded magazines.

* * *

Back at the hotel I had a lot of things on my mind. I was really excited about the multifaceted adventure that was panning out before me. On the one hand, there was the heart pounding thrill of a possible "love" interest. On the other hand, there was the heart stopping excitement about what we were going to experience with both Company B and the law enforcement folks.

Anyway, Tyler had told me, since the summer term didn't start until the following week, she was working "normal duty hours" at the Five and Dime. She usually got home around a quarter to six. With my heart in my throat, I dialed her number at six o'clock. My heart stopped when I heard Tyler's mesmerizing voice on the other end of the phone. I was asked if I planned to go to church on Sunday. "Of course," I answered. Would I, Tyler asked, like to accompany she and her brother to Mass. If so, would I have any trouble getting on base to go to the base chapel? No problem, I said, I had both a military identification card and a journalist pass.

CHAPTER THREE

"a time for war . . ."
Ecclesiastes 3: 8

O ur time at Camp Bullis turned out to be a blast. Keeping thoughts of Miss Devine and the communist activists in the back of my mind, I really got into the Marine drill. It brought back a lot of neat memories. To start with, we had to leave Austin with the convoy at 0500 for the ninety-mile drive to Camp Bullis Army National Guard Training Center. One of the lesser pleasures of military life that is not to be missed is a ride in a Deuce and a Half. These large trucks are the work-horses of the service. They are hot in the summer and cold in the winter. Crammed in on top of other Marines, the ride is stiff, uncomfortable and features roaring engine and wind noise. You also get the never-ending pungent odor of diesel exhaust. It struck me as funny how much I had missed it.

For the longest time I had planned on being a career Marine. I had enlisted back in 1957 and busted my butt to be a good Marine. My performance led to acceptance into the Platoon Leaders Course at Quantico, Virginia. Discharged into the Reserves to attend College, I was accepted by St. Edward's University in Austin. St. Edward's was known as the Notre Dame of the South because it too, like Indiana's Notre Dame had been founded in 1877 by Father Ed Sorin in honor of his patron saint, St. Edward, King and Confessor. After receiving my commission an unfortunate injury sustained during jungle warfare training in Panama limited my value to the Corps. I was assigned to Company B as part of the active-duty cadre and later transitioned into reserve status.

It never ceases to amaze me how we do things in the Marines. We joke among ourselves that USMC stands for Uncle Sam's misguided children. The Corps, as some of us saw it, was an institution of great tradition almost 200 years old, unhampered by progress. But tradition is a good thing.

Wednesday's schedule called for refresher training in self-aid/buddy care and fire team and small squad tactics. Thursday would be really grueling and Friday was just scheduled to be a day at the range and return home.

Thursday's planned field exercises had Company B scheduled to set up fire bases on three separate hilltops in a single day's time. With the advent of modern airlift, you'd think the big gray Boeing CH-46 Sea Knights would swoop in and airlift us from one hill top to the next. Nope, instead, on the cusp of a Texas summer, the company had to climb each steep hill in the sweltering heat and humidity. Then, after we had gotten the fire base established, a platoon was left behind to man it. The helicopters then airlifted us to the next targeted "deep" valley so we could set out again to climb the next Mt. Everest. Seems to me, we could have saved a lot of time, and energy if the choppers would have just taken us from one hill top to the next.

The day could not have been any better. Being around Marines again, the excitement of the chopper rides and the physical exertion were fantastic. I had a job to do so I had to keep my thoughts on the seriousness of the assignment. Marines were fighting and dying in an increasingly unpopular war overseas and more and more people were showing less and less respect for the men and women who go into harm's way on their behalf. When we got dropped off for our last hill ascent, I watched the "grunts" jump out of the back of the aircraft, I thought of Sacred Scripture, Psalm 144 and 1st Samuel to be specific. "Blessed be the Lord my Rock who trains my hands for battle, my fingers for war" and "it is not by the sword or spear that the Lord saves, for the battle is the Lord's."

The men of Company B were in the truest sense, citizen soldiers. They were every day guys, just weekend warriors as some sarcastically call them. There were a couple of guys like me who were school teachers. There were truck drivers, electricians, plumbers, mail carriers, college students and store clerks. The First Sergeant was a professor who taught Economics at the University of Texas. Chances were, as reservists, they would never be mobilized and sent into combat. But there was always the possibility. People who take an oath to put it all on the line for others are heroes to me because, as the Alamo's Colonel William Travis put it, they're willing to fight for "liberty, patriotism and everything dear to the American character." I have always believed service before self was a core value. I believed, as Colonel Travis did, we have a duty to fight and when necessary, "die like a soldier who never forgets what is due to honor and that of his country."

That night I enjoyed the C Rations, camp coffee, and sleep under the stars. The canned beans and meatballs, circa 1952 were great. I had forgotten how much I liked the huge, fudge covered graham cracker cookie that some call a "silver dollar," others call a "John Wayne." The coffee was "grunt strong" and good but my sleeping bag smelled too much like moth-balls.

Friday was not that physically taxing because we spent its entirety at the firing range. Company B had recently been issued new M-16 semi-automatic/automatic weapons to replace its old M-14s. The M-16s were much lighter and more lethal than the M-14s. Marines qualify once a year on a course with human size targets 500 meters down range. Even though the men of Company B were reservists and get little of the range time active duty folks get, they still shot remarkably well. Enemies of America be advised. Don't mess with Marine riflemen, even those that are weekend warriors.

About 1500, after a box lunch of hot milk, bologna and cheese sandwiches and Hostess Twinkies, Hitch and I were told it was time for us to saddle up and move out for the return to Austin. Talk about having a sense of anticipation, I was excited and anxious at the same time.

Fifty miles per hour is about the best you can expect in a Deuce and a Half. It took over an hour to get to the rest area between San Antonio and San Marcos. As we left Highway 35, I noticed the roadside park wasn't as crowded as it usually was on Friday afternoons. It was odd that a fruit stand selling watermelons was over by the commercial truck parking. Just as odd, the only other vehicle in the neighborhood was a panel truck marked "Cloud Soft Linen Service."

The convoy pulled into the truck parking area and all the vehicles were shut down. Hitch and I looked on from the ambulance parked in back of the pack. Instead of 130 Marines jumping out of the trucks and running in mass to the rest rooms, nothing happened. I think that confused the villains. After a few moments, the fruit stand vendors, three in all, grabbed AK47 assault weapons from the watermelon crates. They started for the Company Commander. Nearly at the same time, two others emerged from the panel truck with their weapons.

In the blink of an eye, I heard a Texas Department of Public Safety helicopter. Canvas covers on the rear of the trucks came down and an over whelming force of Special Weapons and Tactics personnel from the joint Texas Ranger and FBI team jumped out and pounced upon the bad guys. It was all over in a matter of five minutes. Not a shot was fired and no one was injured. Thank God I thought, the anti-American fanatics were not fanatic enough to take their own lives in a losing fight. Both Hitch and I were really impressed with the professionalism and precision of the law enforcement folks. They also take an oath to support and defend the Constitution. They too put their lives on the line every day, every minute for America. We owe them a debt of gratitude too. Hitch took photos and was careful to avoid shots that would lead to the recognition of the heroes.

Before the convoy pulled out, a Department of Public Safety Public Affairs official out briefed us and told us what we could and couldn't say and report about the incident. Concerned about compromising other on-going operations, they wanted final approval of our report and pictures before going to press. That wouldn't be a problem, we assured them.

*   *   *

I had trouble sleeping that Friday night. I was way too geared up from the excitement of the week. My mind jumped from one thing to another, meeting Tyler, the drill, the attack by the communist fanatics, getting to see Tyler again. Then Saturday seemed to crawl by.

When Sunday morning finally came, I was as giddy as a school boy. I was looking forward to making a good impression on Tyler and her brother. But I had a problem. With all the excitement of the week I had forgotten to get my sport jackets and slacks cleaned and pressed. Since I travelled light, I had limited choices. There was the dark blue sport jacket and khaki slacks and then there was the black sport jacket and khaki slacks. At the last minute it dawned on me that I had a third option. Hitch and I were about the same size. I recalled He had arrived at the airport wearing a nice light brown camel hair sport coat. I went by his room and grabbed it from him.

Like most United States Air Force installations, Randolph AFB is a very scenic, well maintained and manicured facility. The base is another example why the Air Force gets the nod as the Cadillac of services. The base chapel was an attractive white building with twin towers like those chapels built in the Spanish colonial period. It was similar to the Concepcion and San Jose Mission's back in town.

I met Tyler and her brother near the entrance. Tyler wore a light, sleeveless summer dress with the same cute white turquoise studded western boots. I couldn't help but notice how the sun light streamed through the fringes of Tyler's white dress to give it a translucence that was exquisitely revealing. Her brother Travis was much taller and a ruddy faced, outdoorsy looking young man. After handing Tyler a yellow rose, I shook hands with Travis.

Tyler seemed to be happy to see me. Travis seemed to be sizing me up. I knew I was going to be evaluated by both. I said a silent prayer that I'd be found worthy enough to take Tyler on a date or two.

Friday's incident had made the evening news. The DPS public affairs spokesman had said that a couple of journalists from a Christian magazine had been with the convoy. Tyler and Travis took that to mean Hitch and I and they both expressed their happiness that we were not harmed.

When we sat together in the pew, Travis sat between us. All the while there was a vibrant and distracting fragrance of vanilla spice in the air. It was the most uncomfortable time I had ever spent in church.

Afterward, I followed them in my rental car to Bill Miller Bar B Q for brunch. Travis and Tyler sat side by side across from me. The food I'm sure was good but at that time I couldn't taste anything. Too uptight I was trying to make a good impression on both sister and brother. Initially I thought it was in my favor that Travis was intent on being a "mustang" like me, that is an enlisted guy that earns his way up the ladder to get a commission. Travis aimed to be an officer in the Air Force while I was already a 1st Lieutenant in the USMCR.

Travis had a lot of questions that got to the heart of "who" I was as a person. I could tell he had performed such interrogations many times. He was good at it and good at weaving questions between those that dealt with me with inquiries about the state of Colorado and the city of Colorado Springs. Then it happened. Travis sat erect and pushed his chair back a little. "In all seriousness," he said, "I was worried about you being an older, big city guy and all. You know Mister Taylor, when your younger sister is . . ."

I stopped Travis in mid-sentence and asked him to call me Josh. I then tried to assure him that I was a man of character, especially when it came to women.

"I appreciate what you're saying Josh but when your younger sister is a small-town girl that looks like this," Travis made an exaggerated gesture of pointing at Tyler, "you can't be too careful. But I think I like you. I think maybe you're alright."

Without another word being said, in the swiftest and most graceful way possible, Tyler sprang to her feet and came around the table and sat down beside me. I couldn't tell you how special that moment made me feel but I can tell you the fragrance of vanilla spice nearly knocked me off my chair. The barbecue actually turned out to taste good and I wished we could have spent more time together, but Tyler had to get to work at the BX. I almost forgot to act my age after Tyler and I settled on a plan to meet midweek at the base bowling alley.

*　　*　　*

Our first or second date, depending on how you looked at it, happened early in the evening on Wednesday. Tyler wore a pair of jeans she had just purchased. She was concerned they looked too tight on her. I told her the jeans looked just right. Tyler also wore an oversize baggy Southwest Texas State sweat shirt and a well weathered Houston Astro baseball cap. When she put her bowling shoes on, I was struck by how dainty her little feet were. Cute they were too in her little pink, ankle length socks. Her ankles were pretty too. I scored pretty poorly because I was so enamored of Tyler. She was a good bowler, usually scoring about 130. And, I couldn't believe the way she seemed to be enjoying my company.

Tyler had an adorable childlike side. Each frame, as she prepared to walk up to the line, she'd rotate her ball cap 180 degrees and come to attention. Holding the ball with both hands, she'd raise it to waist level and stomp her right foot twice. Then Tyler would gracefully proceed to the line and throw the ball down the lane. While the ball was in transit, she clinched her fists and leaned to the left or right as necessary in an attempt to influence the trajectory of the ball. If she scored well, she kind of skipped back to her seat. If she scored poorly, she returned with the cutest pout and flop herself down. It was all so endearing.

When we took a break for hamburgers at the grill, Tyler told me about the first time she had tried to bowl. She was probably around four and a half and her father had her kneel down at the line. He placed a ball in front of her and told her to give it a shove and try to knock down a couple of pens. Tyler laughed with her eyes welling up a bit in tears. "It went about two feet and then right into the gutter. But I think that's why I love to bowl. I'm reminded of my dad."

It warmed my heart to think that Tyler would open up to me like that. Walking back to our lane, I became self-conscious of the way some guys looked at her. Most I was sure were just admiring God's handiwork, but I worried that there were probably some predators looking on too. At most 5' 3" and likely no more than 120 pounds if soaked to the bones from standing in the rain, Tyler needed protection. Like her brother, I felt a strong desire to look out for her too.

Late in the evening I mustered the courage to ask Tyler if I could see her again. She said she was free Sunday because the Exchange would be closed for inventory. I asked her if we could meet again for Mass and then maybe go up to Austin to visit a couple sites I frequented in college. She said she would be delighted to do that.

*   *   *

Once again, I met Tyler and her brother out in front of the Chapel. As she thanked me for the yellow-rose I handed her, Travis chimed in, "what, nothing for me?" Tyler was dressed in a little pink dress that stopped well above her pretty knees. Her white turquoise studded western boots looked good with that dress too.

Tyler's stunning red hair was tied back with a big pink ribbon. This time, she and I sat next to each other. I remember hoping the Good Lord would forgive me for being a bit distracted. I fought with myself the whole time to keep from looking down at her beautiful legs. The fragrance of vanilla spice was also wonderfully distracting.

Austin's Zilker Park and the Barton Springs pool are two must see places in Austin, Texas. When I had been in college, I had spent a lot of leisure time in both places. And, every six months the Marine Corps Reserve Unit conducted its physical fitness evaluations there. That had always been a neat experience, 130 plus Marines running all around the park doing set-ups, pull ups and the three-mile run. Hundreds of other civilians who were out and about in the park always seemed to get a kick out of what we were doing.

The Barton Springs pool is a nice three-acre spring fed swimming area surrounded by a luscious green lawn and lots of trees. There is a small dam at the western end that usually diverts Barton Creek away from the pool. As

27

Tyler and I sat next to each other at a picnic table drinking Dr. Pepper, Tyler told me about the time her aunt had brought the family up from Yoakum on the 4th of July weekend. At the time, recent thunderstorms had caused Barton Creek to overflow the dam and there was a strong current out in the middle of the pool. Tyler got herself caught in the current and couldn't get out. Thrashing around, being wildly tossed around in the current, she had gone under several times and badly gashed her knee. Swallowing lots of water, she got really, really scared and thought she was going to drown. In telling the story, Tyler got choked up and misty eyed. Had Travis not come to her rescue, she said in a trembling voice, she would have been "a goner."

After a moment or two, Tyler got her composure back. Smiling, she pointed down at her knee at the long six- or seven- inch scar on its side. For a brief moment she seemed like a little girl. Grinning, Tyler said, "see my battle scar? There was blood everywhere. We spent three hours in emergency over at St. David's Hospital, tons of stitches."

"Thank God for Travis," I said to her. "What a gorgeous knee," I said to myself.

Rummaging through her western style, turquoise studded tote bag, Tyler liked turquoise a lot, she took out a little black binder that had photographs in it. "I take this with me whereever I go. I think I'm kind of nostalgic." Tyler opened the book to a little 3X5 black and white photo she said was taken just before the accident. She and Travis stood in front of the very same tree that was next to our picnic table. Speaking before thinking, "Nice bathing suit," I said. I think that embarrassed Tyler. She looked down and said, "Thank you."

In the photograph, Tyler was a pretty sixteen-year-old young lady. I took note of how, in the years since, she had filled out well in all the right places. I'm sure I blushed at the thought. Tyler then took great delight in showing me some other photos. There were the photographs of her parents including one of her father dressed in what we called "Dress Greens." She was proud of the photo of Travis in his baseball uniform. It was taken after he had thrown a 3 hitter to beat their hated rival, Victoria High School. Tyler got especially animated when she showed me the photo of her Aunt holding "Miss Whiskers," their little tabby kitten.

After Tyler returned her photos to her bag, I asked her, "how is it that you haven't been snatched up by some strong athletic type?"

Tyler seemed to get contemplative. She turned serious. "I've gone out with more than my fair share of guys but by the second date I'd know, they weren't right for me."

"So," I asked, "you've never gone out with anybody more than twice?"

"That's right." she said.

I tried to calibrate in my mind where I stood with the fetching young Texan. I thought, if you count the Sunday brunch, the outing at the bowling alley and this trip to Austin, we've been out three times. "So then," I asked with a grin on my face, "third time's a charm?"

I think Tyler picked up on what I was getting at. She got up from the table and started walking down the path. A few paces from the picnic table, she stopped, looked over her shoulder and beamed a big smile, "Maybe," she answered.

Feeling encouraged I jumped up and joined her. After we had walked from the shade into the open area of the park, it dawned on me that the heat and humidity might be too uncomfortable for Tyler. I asked her if she'd like to go somewhere else. She said she was enjoying our walk.

After a few minutes of quiet, I looked down at Tyler's white turquoise studded western boots. "Aren't those uncomfortable to be walking around in?" I asked.

Tyler looked over at me and laughed her sweet, sweet sounding Texas accented laugh, "We Texans wear our boots to do everything."

"Everything?" I asked. Tyler was incredulous. She answered emphatically, "Everything!" But before we had taken another step, she added a modifier, "Everything except bowl." We both laughed.

A few more minutes of silence passed between us and then Tyler started asking questions of a spiritual nature.

"Tell me Josh, you have a favorite Psalm?"

"Sure do," I answered. "Since I love the mountains, the 121st has always been my favorite." I started to recite it and only got the first few words in before Tyler joined in and we both prayed it aloud.

"I look to the mountains,
From where does my help come?
It comes from the Lord who made Heaven and earth
He will not let you stumble
He who watches over you never slumbers,
Indeed, He who watches over Israel
never slumbers or sleeps.
The Lord Himself watches over you
And stands beside you as your protective shield,
The sun will not harm you by day
Nor the moon by night.
The Lord keeps you from all harm and evil
The Lord watches your coming and going,
Both now and forever."

Again, we laughed. I thought to myself; "How neat is this? This young lady actually knows Scripture." Turn about being fair play, I then asked Tyler what her favorite Psalm was. Without hesitation she said the 27th. As she had done with me, I joined her in saying the psalm after she had spoken just a few words.

"The Lord is my light and my salvation
Whom should I fear.
The Lord is my life's refuge
Of what should I be afraid.
When evil doers come at me
To devour my flesh,
They, themselves stumble and fall.
Though an army encamp against me
My heart does not fear

Though war be waged against me
Even then do I trust.
One thing I ask of the Lord,
This I seek
To dwell in the House of the Lord
All the days of my life
To gaze on the Lord's beauty
To visit His Temple
For God will hide me in His Shelter
In time of trouble,
He will conceal me in the cover of His Tent
And set me high upon a rock.
Even now my head is held high
Above my enemies on every side!
I will offer in His Tent
Sacrifices with shouts of joy
I will sing and chant praise to the Lord."

Once more we found humor in our shared love of Scripture. As we continued our walk around the park, I thought again about how everything about Tyler was so endearing. Sure, her beauty could cause a man to be simply infatuated with her. But Tyler also had an aura about her. She had an interior beauty of soul and spirit that effervesced to the surface to accentuate her natural, physical beauty. Surely the Good Lord had to be pleased with Tyler's palpable spiritual centeredness. You could sense she had a personal relationship with God. "Man, oh man," I thought. "Tyler is something else. She's a real spiritual powerhouse."

The next thing to ask Tyler, I thought, was a natural follow-on. What was her favorite Scripture passage? Tyler had grown up believing the Good Lord wanted us to accept Him as a personal Savior whom we can lean on every day. Because she believed the Lord was always calling out to us, she had always liked a specific passage from St. Matthew. I joined in again after she had spoken just a few words.

"Come to Me all you who are weary and heavy burdened
And I will give you rest,
Take My yoke upon you and learn from Me,
For I am meek and humble of heart
And you will find rest for your souls,
For My yoke is easy and My burden light."

In answer to the same question, Because I like eagles and have done a lot of physically demanding stuff in my time, I have always related to a particular passage in Isaiah. This too, Tyler knew by heart.

"Do you not know, have you not heard?
The Lord God Almighty is the Creator of all things.
He never grows tired and His ways are unfathomable.
He gives strength to the weak
And power to the powerless.
Even though young men grow weary and faint
And youths stagger and fail,
They that wait upon the Lord will renew their strength.
They will mount up with wings as eagles.
They will run and not grow weary.
They will walk and not grow faint."

"OK then," Tyler stopped in her tracks, "what's your favorite Book in the Bible?"

Slightly embarrassed, I hesitated for a slight moment because I didn't want to reveal just how much of a romantic at heart I was. I told her, "The Book of Tobit."

"Why?" she asked.

"Because the Book of Tobit has everything you would want in a good story. It has adventure and romance. "What's your favorite?"

Tyler smiled a cute half smile, half grin, "The Book of Esther," she said, "and for the same reasons."

After we started walking again, I asked her how she had gotten so well versed in Scripture. Tyler said her aunt would have them sit in the living room for at least 15 minutes every night and take turns reading out loud from the Holy Bible. She said it usually took them about a year and a half to go through all 73 Books, from Genesis to Revelation.

When the path around the park began to parallel Town Lake, I noticed how nearly placid the water was, there were just slight ripples. Close to the bank, in addition to the reflection of the impressive Austin skyline, I saw Tyler's image too. The light ripples in the water gave her image an ethereal quality. I smiled at myself remembering what I had thought when she walked away from me in the little café back in San Antonio.

*   *   *

Near the end of our stroll we passed a young couple seated on a bench. They were locked in a passionate embrace. Two steps later I felt Tyler's hand in mine. Our pace slowed considerably. I didn't want the walk to end. We said nothing for the longest time. Holding hands is no big thing but it is a big thing. I was euphoric. It must have met something to Tyler too or she wouldn't have done it.

Some years back it had taken me a little over 19 minutes to run the three-mile course around Zilker Park. That had been my last Marine Corps fitness test. It had taken Tyler and I well over two hours to walk the same path. Maybe she did like my company. Granted, we had just met, but maybe, I thought, we could be one of those matches made in Heaven.

*   *   *

Tyler's playful, even maybe what you'd call a wild side emerged during our return to San Antonio. Tammy Wynette's "Your Good Girl's Gonna Go Bad" came on the radio and Tyler asked if she could turn the volume up. Before I could say anything, the radio was louder and Tyler was bouncing about, playfully singing along. She had a beautiful voice that nearly mimicked the country singer, albeit with a noticeable Texas twang. While she sang the up-beat song, Tyler shook her head left and right, right and left. Her ravishing long red hair went this way and that.

At the refrain Tyler looked up into the mirror and pretended to get painted up and powdered up. Singing along with the song, she traced her lips and eyelids with her fingers and then patted her cheeks. During the short two-minute duration of the whimsical song, Miss Devine may not have really become a good girl gone bad but she was definitely the swingingest young lady I had ever seen. When the song ended, Tyler turned down the volume and snickered. "Sorry but I really like that song."

I told her I didn't mind it a bit.

*　　*　　*

After shaking hands and bidding Travis a cordial farewell, Tyler showed me to the door. She knew I was leaving for San Diego the next morning so I nervously asked her if we could stay in touch. She said nothing. She stood up on her tip toes, put her arms around my neck, leaned up and gave me a quick kiss. Again, she said nothing.

Driving back to the hotel, a thousand things ran through my mind. Talk about bittersweet, I said to myself. The day had been filled with remarkable peaks of excitement and joy and had come to an end on the worse downer ever. Tyler's mood had changed 180 degrees in the short span of time from when I opened her car door and we got to her apartment. It wasn't going to be the match made in Heaven I had hoped for. Tyler was a very special lady and I hoped the best for her. Maybe someday, I thought, we'd run into each other up in the Springs.

*　　*　　*

The next morning, Hitch and I returned our rental car and headed for the Western Airlines ticket counter. I wasn't looking forward to the air travel because there would be too much idle time to sit and think. As we approached the counter, I saw Tyler. My heart leaped into my throat.

I didn't know what to say. Once again, a thousand thoughts popped into my head.

Tyler smiled. "Josh, I didn't want you to leave before I gave you an answer to your question."

Right away I realized what she was referring to. Thinking quickly to myself, I thought the answer must be in the affirmative or she wouldn't have fought the early morning traffic to get to the airport. "And the answer is?" I asked.

Tyler handed me a yellow rose and said she'd like us to stay in touch. "Maybe," she asked, "if you can find the time, could you please give me a call tonight?"

Taking the rose from her soft, small, pretty hand, I noticed her pink colored nail polish. "What time?" I asked.

"1800 Marine time, OK?" she answered. Then, just like she had done the night before, Tyler stepped up on her tip toes, leaned toward me and wrapped her arms around my neck. She leaned up and gave me the longest and sweetest kiss I had ever been given. Slowly pulling away, Tyler whispered, "don't forget to water the rose."

* * *

Hitch was at it again. After we checked our bags and walked to the gate, he kept whistling "The Yellow Rose of Texas."

Instead of dreading the trip that was going to take us all the way north to Salt Lake City, Utah so we could catch another flight that would take us all the way south to San

Diego, I found myself caught up in feelings of excitement and joy. As I sang the song to myself, I found my heart especially captivated by the thought that the yellow rose of Texas might just be the only girl for me.

After a little over two hours in the air to Salt Lake City, we had an hour and a half lay over. We landed in San Diego at three o'clock in the afternoon. It was as I had always found the city, bathed in sunshine. The temperature was about the same as it had been in San Antonio, but with none of the humidity. I got our bags and Hitch got our rental Car.

Actually, the United States Marine Corps Recruit Depot is right next door to the airport, only a small chain link fence separates the two. But, to get to MCRD you have to drive a round-about course to get there. Visitors find the Marine base to be an attractive, well-maintained facility with what I'd call Mediterranean architecture. Established in 1923, there were still plenty of World War Two era Quonset Huts on the periphery of the parade deck. But there were newer recruit squad bays too. Just on the other side of the fence from the airport were the physical training fields, the obstacle course and pugil stick ponds. I made a note of walking past the sandy pit we affectionately called "happy valley."

The United States Marine Corps is considered to be an elite fighting force known for its unique esprit de corps and unrivalled record in combat. It is as old as our nation. It was founded by the Continental Congress on November 10th, 1775, in a tavern in Philadelphia, Pennsylvania.

38

United States Marines fought with John Paul Jones, defeated the pirates of Tripoli, fought alongside Ulysses S. Grant to plant the Stars and Stripes in Mexico City and helped Robert E. Lee arrest John Brown at Harper's Ferry. In World War One, because of their fierce, determined fighting spirit, German soldiers called the Marines "devil dogs." Their performance in World War Two and Korea solidified the reputation of the Corps as being the world's best among the best.

Marine recruit training has historically been between eight and ten weeks in duration. It is divided into three distinct phases. Initial training at MCRD and then rifle marksmanship and basic infantry training up the road at Camp Pendleton. Recruit training, through its "artificial high stress environment" separates the men from the boys, the "hackers from the non-hackers." The days of training are filled with academics, physical fitness training, marching and weapon close order drill. The duty day starts with reveille at 0500 and ends with taps at 2130.

One of the proudest days in the life of those of us who have undergone the crucible is when you graduate from bootcamp and are called a Marine for the first time.

*   *   *

Hitch and I were met at the Visiting Officer Quarters by 1st Lieutenant Dabney "Dab" Stewart and an old friend, Father Jerry O'Mahony, Commander, United States Navy. After exchanging pleasantries, we set out for our first stop, the recruit receiving area in a tiny courtyard. Just as we arrived, an olive-green bus pulled up. Thirty or so former civilians were quickly herded off the vehicle and ordered to stand on a series of yellow painted footprints with heals touching and toes at forty-five-degree angles.

As we looked on, a picture-perfect Marine Drill Instructor walked down the steps from the Barber Shop. Speaking in a booming and commanding voice, Staff Sergeant Glenn Lodge gave the newbies instructions on the first fundamental of military bearing and behavior, the proper position of attention. Then the young men were filed into the barber shop to partake of another fundamental tradition of the United States Marine Corps.

Hitch and I looked on and quietly laughed to ourselves. We were reliving a memory never forgotten. For both of us, we had lived the experience firsthand not more than a decade ago. While his new charges were occupied, SSgt. Lodge was introduced to us. He was pleased to know that we too were members of the fraternity. We told him we had a lot of respect for men like him. SSgt. Lodge and his fellow instructors had only weeks to do what most parents had failed to do, make a man out of "junior." Besides doing that, the Drill Instructors had to instill in the former civilians the gung-ho spirit the Corps is famous for. If recruits learned well, they left MCRD with the basic warrior and survivor skills needed to be "life-takers" and not "crow bait."

After a bit of small talk, Hitch and I left for the VOQ to get cleaned up. Glenn Lodge, Dab Stewart, Father Jerry, Hitch and I were to meet later at a scheduled get together at 1800 in the Officer's Club.

*   *   *

40

I had forgotten that San Antonio was two hours ahead of California. I gave Tyler a call at 1700 my time, 1900 her time. I was annoyed that an old guy like me should get nervous about talking to a young lady. Happily, Tyler answered straightaway and I apologized, saying I had forgotten to ask her if she had met for me to call her at 1800 her time or 1800 my time. The sweet, disarming chuckle on the other end of the phone quickly put me at ease. She admitted that she too had forgotten about the time zone difference.

We talked for nearly an hour. All the while I looked at the yellow rose Tyler had given me. I had gotten a tiny crystal vase for it over at the BX. I felt Tyler smiling on the other end of the phone as she told me about talking things over with her brother. She told Travis that when she prayed about whether or not to see me again, she got the notion that I might be the right guy for her. Travis was supportive of us starting a relationship. He resaid what he had at Bill Miller Bar B Q. He liked me and thought I was OK.

My spirit soared. I felt as light as a feather. As I was answering Tyler's questions about how our day had been, I heard her door bell ring. A few moments later I heard Travis say that the dozen yellow roses I had wired during our Salt Lake layover had arrived. Tyler's voice cracked as she softly thanked me for the roses. She said she'd like to get together again as soon as we could. We planned to talk again the next night.

*   *   *

The Prime Rib and baked potato were very enjoyable. The Officer Club was known for good food and good service. The purpose of the meeting was to get a "boots on the ground" input on the spiritual and philosophical aspects of military service. To end the evening, we'd get an update on the current military situation.

In the receiving area in the small courtyard there is a sign painted in bright scarlet and gold that reads, "To be a Marine, you have to believe in yourself, your fellow Marine, your Corps, your Country and your God. Semper Fidelis."

Semper Fidelis is Latin for "always faithful" and it is the motto of the Marine Corps. Father Jerry spoke to the Biblical connotation of the motto in that the Good Lord is always faithful to us and He expects us to be faithful to Him too. For the true patriot, such fidelity extends to one's commitment to "duty, honor, country." In elaborating, Father Jerry referenced the Book of Genesis, "the Lord took man and settled him in the Garden of Eden to cultivate it and care for it." "In a similar sense," Father Jerry went on, "we have been given America to cultivate and care for too."

Father Jerry then went into Church teaching. The 4th Commandment obviously obligates us to honor our parents. But the Church also holds it obligates us to love our country. That is because, as St. Thomas Aquinas put it, our existence and guidance in life come from God but our parents and country play a part too. That being the case, citizens, Father Jerry stressed, "should have a generous and loyal spirit of patriotism. As the Book of Nehemiah says, we have a duty to fight for our brethren, our sons and daughters, our wives and our homes."

Don't forget, Father Jerry added, "the Lord Himself told us to sell our cloak and buy a sword if we don't have one. I think that means He expects us to be prepared to fight when it's morally justified." "And in that vein," said Father Jerry, "the Church holds that those who serve faithfully in the armed services are great contributors to the common good because they protect freedom, provide security and help maintain peace."

Then most surprisingly, SSgt. Glenn Lodge, the battle-hardened veteran, a Purple Heart recipient who had been twice deployed to South Vietnam brought up the topic of "love." "God tells us we are required to love Him with our whole heart, soul, mind and strength. Then He tells us we're obligated to love our neighbor. All the Commandments, the Lord said are wrapped up in these two things." The hard corps veteran then got emotional, "Just because there are 8,000 miles and a large ocean separating us, that doesn't make the people of South Vietnam any less our neighbors. And those neighbors are as entitled to freedom and self-determination as we are."

SSgt. Lodge continued, "I've dedicated my life to the Profession of Arms. In our fallen, imperfect world, like the Bible says, there are times when it is morally justified and absolutely necessary 'to kill and tear things down'. Granted, we can't go everywhere to be an enforcer but when we can and we should, we need to fight. And one of those times is when, like God says in Leviticus, our neighbor's life is at stake."

Father Jerry pounded his fist on the table, fortunately not enough to spill anything. "Glenn, I couldn't have said it better."

Listening and taking notes on what Father Jerry and SSgt. Lodge had to say brought my mind back to when I had enlisted. I remembered how it hadn't taken long for me to realize that many of my fellow recruits were not as patriotic and idealistic as I was. They had other reasons for being there. Some just wanted to get away from home and find steady work. Others just wanted the educational benefits or occupational training the military offered. A few were there because, as they told me, they really had little choice. They had either been drafted or arrested for various crimes and offered the choice of either enlisting or going to jail. I think they chose wisely.

To me, United States Marines and their other brothers and sisters in arms are "peace-makers" and the Lord Himself tells us, "blest are the peacemakers."

Father Jerry and the sergeant had done a noble job of speaking to the spiritual and philosophical aspects of military service. Now we'd get to hear an official word from 1st Lieutenant Dab Stewart on the status of current military operations. Hitch and I grinned at each other. We were sympathetic to the Lieutenant's plight because we understood He could only give us a "canned" input for our article.

"The United States military is an instrument of policy. It does not set policy. We admit that the war in South Vietnam is not going well. At present the Johnson Administration and the Defense Department have nearly

70,000 Marines in South Vietnam. There are tens of thousands more Army, Navy and Air Force personnel in the region too." The Lieutenant took a deep breath, then continued.

"As of 1967, major U.S. involvement has been going on for over a year and a half. Of the 11,000 small communities, i.e. hamlets in South Vietnam, far less than half are friendly to U.S. forces. To some observers it was an open question as to whether or not the recent South Vietnamese elections were really fair and open. Combat has been hot and heavy and fortunately we have inflicted five times the number of casualties on the enemy than we have suffered. The United States Marine Corps stands ready to comply with any and all mission taskings we are charged with by our duly elected civilian leaders." Lieutenant Stewart took another breath and grinned, "and gentlemen, that concludes my briefing."

On behalf of Christian Focus magazine, Hitch and I thanked the three men for their time and contribution. Regardless of whether the political decision would be to escalate or reduce American involvement in Southeast Asia, every mother's son at our dinner table agreed the folks at MCRD had a vital mission, that being to ensure that no ghost of any deceased Marine ever returned with the lament, "if only you had done a better job."

*　　*　　*

The Next day, Tuesday, June 13th, Hitch and I got up before reveille so we could be on board for the start of the duty day. We'd be observing SSgt Lodge and his "herd" the whole day. Being an observer of Marine training is a very benign experience when compared with being a participant. Either way you're filled with awe. You see the slogan, "The more you sweat in peace, the less you bleed in war" posted numerous places around MCRD. Marine recruits do a lot of sweating.

On our way back to the VOQ at the end of the day we passed by the special sandy pit known as "happy valley." A platoon that had recently committed an infraction of some sort, e.g. someone had talked in formation, dropped a rifle or turned right when they should have turned left, was being "disciplined" by undergoing a rigorous and lengthy period of calisthenics. As the privates exercised, they were required to shout as loud as humanly possible, "Loyalty and discipline Sir! Loyalty and discipline Sir!" As recruits ourselves, Hitch and I had both spent more than a good amount of time in that pit.

That night at 1800, after another Prime Rib and baked potato dinner, brief aside here, the folks at the Officer's Club really do know how to make a great steak, I returned to the VOQ. I was excited about calling Tyler. My phone rang as I entered the room. She had gotten tired of waiting for my call.

After a day and a half at MCRD, Hitch and I finished the rest of the week up at Camp Pendleton. Marksman-ship training and basic infantry training had not changed a bit since we first experienced it. Even though we were not obligated to comply with the same protocols as the recruits, we practiced the same "water discipline" they had to. Fifteen mile "force marches" in the hot, dusty hills of Camp Pendleton can really dry you out. Two canteens of water are just not enough.

Friday evening found Hitch and I going over our notes and photographs. After a quick hamburger, we both retired to our rooms to rest up for our return trips, Hitch to Oklahoma City, me to Colorado Springs. But before "lights out," I had to talk to Tyler one last time. She and I had talked at length every night. Among my many nightly prayers of thanksgiving was a prayer to thank God for "Ma Bell."

*　　*　　*

We took off from San Diego on schedule. When our Boeing 727 banked steeply I noted how the ocean shimmered brightly in the morning sun. The image reminded me of the kiss Tyler had given me at the airport in San Antonio. That kiss had made my soul shimmer brightly too.

In a matter of moments, the jet leveled off and headed east. The folks at the magazine's head office in Virginia Beach, Virginia had been extremely pleased with my article when I phoned it in late the night before. My job wasn't finished because they requested a piece of prose to close out the feature. The flight home gave me the opportunity to write. I took out my notepad and pen.

"He has to travel far before he can rest. Already many miles have gone underfoot. The weather, the terrain, have not been accommodating. They seldom have. He walks on.

His boots sink deeper into the mud with each step. His jungle utilities are soiled and drenched in the steady downpour. The rain drops hit upon his helmet, ride around its rim then spill over in persistent streams onto his shoulders and back. He walks on.

He loses his footing. He slides and slips as he struggles with himself to find the energy to go on. He forces himself to take one step at a time. He stumbles up the muddy embankment. He sighs. His dirty, unshaven face itches. The blisters on his feet hurt. He is chilled and shivers uncontrollably. His body aches. He walks on.

Tripping, he lands on his M-16 rifle. He pauses momentarily to clean the mud caked in the weapon's flash suppressor. His stomach churns with hunger. His throat is dry. His canteens are empty. The burden of the countless pounds of equipment and provisions riding atop his back becomes heavier with each passing moment. With each step his weariness grows. The hills are steep. His feet are weary. He fights the sleep from his eyes. He walks on.

He is an American fighting man. He doesn't have to be where he is. He knows that. He walks on. He walks on as others have done in the past. Somebody has to do it. Somebody has to care. He walks on, leaving behind Lexington and Yorktown. He's walked the long road from Chancellorsville and Gettysburg. He's left behind Belleau

Woods and the Argonne. He walks on vividly remembering Tarawa and Iwo Jima. It's hard to forget Omaha Beach and Bastogne. He still thinks about Inchon and the Chosin Reservoir. Sadly, he's said a bittersweet goodbye to Khe Sanh and Saigon. He walks on.

He walks on as always. He'd hold his head high if people were looking. He sacrifices a bit of his freedom today that an entire nation will have freedom tomorrow. There are better paying jobs with fewer hassles and fewer pains. There are few jobs as honorable, as noble. He is the keeper of Freedom's Lighthouse. He safeguards its beacon, who's brilliance and resilience are unceasing and shine for all the world to see. He walks on.

He's done his fair share of complaining. He wouldn't be a G.I. if he didn't. At this moment, he does not think about what he is doing or why he is doing it. He's reached that certain stage, he's unquestioning.

Many of the friends with whom he walked are gone. He mourns their absence. Freedom exacts a price. To an extent he finds solace in the words of his leaders. John Kennedy would say, "In your hands my fellow citizens, more than in mine, will rest the final success or failure of our course. Since our country was founded, each generation has been summoned to give testimony to its national loyalty. The graves of young Americans who answered the call to serve surround the globe."

Abraham Lincoln would add, "From these honored dead we take increased devotion to that cause for which they gave the last full measure of devotion, that we here highly resolve that these dead shall not have died in vain, that this nation, under God, shall have a new birth of freedom and that government of the people, by the people, for the people shall not perish from the earth."

He is an American fighting man. He must travel far before he can rest. There are new troubles to be dealt with on the horizon. His is a sacred mission. He is armed and ready, a willing crusader for the causes of liberty and justice. With him and those like him, the world's "last, best hope" will remain the constitutional republic it was conceived to be, a nation under God with liberty and justice for all. He walks on."

CHAPTER FOUR

"a time to dance . . ."
Ecclesiastes 3:4

T he captain had turned on the "fasten seat belt" sign. The aircraft started its descent and the stewardesses were cleaning up the cabin. It looked like an on-time arrival and I was very pleased with that. Tyler and her brother were going to meet me at the airport. It had only been five days since I had last seen her. It felt like forever. My only saving grace was that we had spoken each and every night.

I believed the Good Lord had taken an active interest in our budding romance. Things seemed to naturally fall in place. Travis had "use or lose" leave he wanted to take before entering the Air Force Academy Prep School. Tyler had been able to make arrangements to make up missed school work for her teacher's certification. I had called my friend and principal at Divine Redeemer, Nicki Charles and told her about a talented young graduate I knew who was interested in starting a teaching career. It so happened that the school was in need of a 2nd grade teacher and being a private school, state teacher certification wasn't required. Tyler had a job interview scheduled for Tuesday, the 20th.

I looked out of my cabin window as we hit a series of bad air pockets. That often happens when you're descending altitude over the Rockies. Below I saw snow-capped Pikes Peak and thought how neat it was going to be for Tyler and her brother to see. Tyler had never been to the Rockies. In fact, Tyler had told me she had never been north of Waco. Not only was she an honest to goodness small town girl, she was a "flat-lander." At 14,110 feet, Pike's Peak would be the highest thing Tyler had ever seen and having a "scoop of ice cream" on top would make it even more impressive.

Taking a closer look at what some call "America's Mountain," I thought about the peak being a metaphor for life. Back in 1806, Zebulon Montgomery Pike had been the first white man to lay eyes on the mountain that would bear his name. The young explorer's observation of the peak had been made from about a hundred miles away when he was camped out east on the Arkansas River. As he saw it, the snow-covered mountain was too high, too formidable to be climbed. Thus, in terms of being a metaphor, Pikes Peak was a problem that seemed to be insurmountable. But, just 14 years later in 1820, another young adventurer named Edwin James took a closer look and climbed to the top. With most problems, a closer examination of the details and applied effort usually gets us to a solution.

Anyway, ground level cross winds gave us a bit of concern when we were trying to land. I found myself wondering. Was the feeling that my heart was in my throat caused from the hard landing or was it from the anticipation and excitement I had about seeing Tyler again?

*　　*　　*

I met them at the baggage claim area. As Tyler and I finished a hug, I saw my little five-year-old God-child running toward me. She zigzagged through the crowd like a candidate for the Heisman Trophy. In a heartbeat she opened her arms and launched herself up toward me and I joyfully caught her in my arms.

"Bring me anything Uncle Josh?" Emily asked as she kissed me on my cheek.

I turned to Tyler and Travis and introduced them to Emily, the daughter of my best friends and neighbors, Carmen and Mike Reid. A moment or two later they both emerged from the crowd with Carmen loudly scolding Emily for running like a "banshee" through the crowd. I opened my brief case and handed Emily a couple of little stuffed animals, a bear from California and an armadillo from Texas. Emily's face lit up with the neatest smile. For some reason she couldn't say armadillo so she kept trying to get everyone to look at her "amarillo." "Mama, daddy, look at my amarillo." Tyler thought that was cute.

After introductions, Mike Reid turned to Tyler, "Josh was right, you're a real looker." Carmen grinned and threw a sharp elbow into her husband's side.

Embarrassed as I was, I told Tyler that wasn't exactly how I had described her to the people in my life I considered to be family. Earlier in the week I had told her all about them, how we had been friends for a hand full of years, how the Good Lord had used me to introduce them to the Faith and how the whole family had been baptized a few Easters back. They were church goers. Carmen taught Sunday School. I love Emily as if she were my own daughter which is a good thing since I am her God-father.

It had been decided that Tyler and Travis would stay at my house. The Lord had blessed me with a nice home and it had three bedrooms. Tyler and Carmen hit it off right from the start. It seemed as though Carmen had seen in Tyler the younger sister she had never had and Tyler saw in Carmen the elder sister that it would have been nice to have grown up with.

Tyler and I had planned out a busy week. To start off, Travis wanted to get out to the Air Force Academy to check out the campus before nightfall. After church the next day, Tyler and Carmen were going shopping to outfit Tyler for our camping trip. Tyler had never gone camping and we planned to head up to our cabin late Sunday afternoon.

*　　*　　*

Tyler and I, Mike and Carmen departed for the mountains a little later than planned. With the Reid's along, Travis felt the situation was well chaperoned so he was staying behind to roam around the Academy on his own. Emily was staying the night with her grandparents.

Our cabin was a hundred miles west of the Springs. Tyler was fascinated by the scenery along the narrow, winding two lane road. I had sometimes taken the view for granted. It made me happy that I could share Colorado with Tyler and it pleased me that she was enjoying what she was seeing.

Colorado is a geologist's and geographer's paradise. If you take a satellite's view of the state, it is a big square. Sliced down the center, north to south, you have the Great Plains to the east and a series of basins and ranges to the west. Down in the lower west corner is the Colorado Plateau.

An hour out of Colorado Springs we stopped at the rest area at the summit of Wilkerson Pass, elevation 9507 feet above sea-level. Tyler seemed like a kid in a candy store. She was thrilled by the aspens, the birds and squirrels that seemed to be all over the place. West of Wilkerson Pass lies South Park, the 2nd largest of the four major geologic basins separating the Front Range of the Rocky Mountains from the ranges that lie further west. South Park is an area of a thousand square miles of highland steppe dotted by aspen covered hills. It is literally a place "where the buffalo roam and the deer and the antelope play." Sixty miles directly west is the usually snowcapped Collegiate Range with mountain summits over 14,000 feet. Mt. Harvard is its tallest at 14,420 feet. Mt. Princeton is next at 14,229 and then Mt. Yale at 14,194.

God had blessed us with a bluebird day. There wasn't a cloud in the sky. As she looked west from the Wilkerson

Pass overlook, Tyler, smiled up at me and took my hand into hers. "It's beautiful."

"Not as beautiful as you," I said.

Grinning, Tyler whispered, "thank you."

*　　*　　*

It was well past dinner time when we arrived at the cabin. Tyler leaned forward in her seat as the car emerged from the thick aspen and evergreen lined roadway and turned into a little clearing on the gentle slope of the hillside. Close by, a doe and her fawn were munching on leaves. There on the edge of the clearing was our simple, 500 square foot cabin.

The rustling aspens and swaying branches of the ponderosa pines near the single-story cabin blended into a chorus of nature's music. It has always reminded me of ocean waves breaking on the shore. Birds sang, rabbits scurried here and there and squirrels jumped from tree to tree. I pointed out to Tyler the pretty two-acre spring fed pond, only a stone's throw away but mostly hidden by trees.

Climbing out of the car, Carmen ordered Mike and I "to unload, unpack and square away the area." We complied.

Tyler and Carmen went into the cabin and less than a minute later Tyler came running back out to the car saying how cozy and adorable she thought the place was. Our cabin was nothing to write home about but it was a warm and dry home away from home.

After a hearty meal of grilled corn on the cob, smoked sausage and a side of chilled fruit salad, Tyler and I walked hand in hand up to the clearing on top of the hill. By the time we had finished dinner, the sun had gone down. At 9200 feet the temperature drops off quick so I had given Tyler my old, but warm Marine field jacket. The jacket was way too big for her. It made her look smaller than she was. Her hands didn't even reach the cuffs of the jacket. She looked like an Eskimo, a really, really cute Eskimo.

When we got to the top of the hill, I turned and pointed up at the Big Dipper and North Star. Tyler stepped to the front and leaned her back into me. She reached back and took my arms and wrapped them around her waist.

Looking up at the velvety, star-studded sky with its tiny wisps of Milky Way, Tyler whispered what I had often heard her say, "It's beautiful."

Then I said to Tyler what she had often heard me say, "Not as beautiful as you." After thanking me again for the compliment, Tyler asked;

"How about a game of prose?"

I didn't hear the question because all of a sudden, I became lost in the moment. The vanilla spice fragrance, the chill of the evening, the soft orange glow from the oil lamp in the cabin window, the smell of the aspen logs from the chimney, holding Tyler like I was under God's breathtaking tapestry of stars was almost too much to take in.

Tyler asked again, "How about a game of prose? You pick the subject and give it a whirl."

I had not "played prose" since my last English class. That had been a long time ago. In the word game, a topic is chosen and the player's take turns adding a sentence or phrase. The loser is the first one to get stumped and the winner is the one that comes up with an unbeatable line that can't be topped.

Looking up, it wasn't hard to pick the subject. I gently rested my chin on Tyler's pink stocking cap that covered her pretty head. Looking up, I began; "Stars, stars, have you ever paused to look at the stars in the sky on a moonless night?"

Tyler quickly added; "There are bright ones and dim ones and seemingly capricious ones that can't make up their mind."

I had an easy follow-on; "They shine brilliantly for a moment and then flicker into a state of near obscurity."

Tyler pondered but a brief moment, then offered; "I've looked at the stars. I've seen and understood."

Only one thought popped into my head; "We are not alone."

Tyler, quick on her feet added; "Emmanuel, God is with us."

Thinking I had her and victory was at hand, I said; "And it was He who made the stars and set them in the dome of the sky to shed light upon the earth, to govern the night and to separate the light from darkness."

Tyler's knowledge of Scripture did me in. She added the proper ending; "And God saw that it was good, evening came and morning followed the 4th Day."

I definitely couldn't top that. I got choked up. The words, "And God saw that it was good" struck a chord with me and took on added meaning. As I squeezed Tyler even tighter in the stillness of the beautiful starry night, I thought, "And God saw that it was good."

Tyler turned around and looked up at me. The tears in her eyes made them sparkle in the star light. I took off her cap and ran my fingers through her lush hair. Speaking before thinking, I said for the first time, "I love you."

Tyler rested her head on my chest and threw her arms around me. She pulled me tight. "I love you too," she said.

We hugged for the longest time. Eventually our embrace took on the nature of a very slow dance. With Heaven above, it was as if Tyler and I gently swayed to the soft, romantic music played by the angelic musicians in the celestial orchestra. I knew I was being rash but I decided right then and there I was going to ask Tyler to marry me. I knew just how I was going to do it too. Losing track of time, I had the same feeling I experienced toward the end of our phone calls. It had been "high-schoolish" but neither one of us wanted to be the first to hang up. Now, neither one of us wanted to be the first to let go.

*   *   *

Tyler's job interview had gone well. My friend and principal at Divine Redeemer Catholic School, Nicki Charles, offered her the 2nd Grade teaching position. She would start the Fall term with me on Tuesday, the 5th of September. Using that as an excuse to go out to celebrate with Travis, Carmen and Mike, we went to a café in Old

Colorado City that was also a venue for folk music. The "Back Shelf" was a quaint little place noted for catering to a more sedate, less rowdy type of crowd. It was a comfortable place to kick back and unwind.

Earlier in the day, since I respected Travis' role as head of their family, I pulled him aside. I told Him how I felt about his sister. He hoped I wasn't rushing things but He shook my hand vigorously and said he was happy for both of us.

The featured group that evening was Ted Sherman and the Atlanta Barn Burners. I had told Tyler that I occasionally dabbled in the music arts and Ted and his group were the guys I usually sang with. After performing a few standards like "Tom Dooley" and "Cotton Fields," Ted called me up to the stage and introduced me to the crowd of about 40 people. "Those of you who are regulars recognize Josh Taylor. He's here tonight to sing a special song to a special lady."

I had to swallow really hard to clear my throat. Ted nodded to his back up. The music started and Ted and I shortly joined in with our harmonized vocals. Truth be told, Ted and I would have never been mistaken for Simon and Garfunkel but we were better than just tolerable. Some might even have said we were quite decent. We sang;

"Be mine tonight and every night
As I go through life in the light of Jesus Christ
Take my hand and walk with me into His light
Be my wife

Life has many paths that we must take
If you're with me, we'll find the narrow gate
God is love and love is all we really need
Hear my plea

Winter I see your face in every snow flake
Summer I hear your voice in the rustling the aspens make
It seems to me our love is meant to be
Stay with me

Be mine tonight and every night
As I go through life in the light of Jesus Christ
Take my hand and walk with me into His light
Be my wife."

In a few minutes it was over. I was pleasantly surprised at the ovation we got. My heart seemed to be beating outside my chest. When I returned to our table, Tyler stood up and hugged me. Stepping up on her tip toes, she leaned up and kissed me, this time playfully biting my lower lip as she stepped back.

Smiling, Tyler said she had a question and a comment. My heart was really in my throat. "The question?"

"What snowflakes?"

"OK, I get it, it's summer time," I forced a smile, "I was just trying to make a point. "and the comment?"

With scarlet lips, pearly white teeth, and sparkling eye's, Tyler's smile brought a brightness to the dimly lit room. Playing off my proposal, she said, "Be my husband."

Ted and I had a prearrangement that if the answer turned out to be an affirmative one, I'd give him a thumbs up. The Barn Burners quickly threw in a little addendum.

They sang "The Yellow Rose of Texas." Then, out came the bus boy with the dozen yellow roses I had also pre-arranged. At that point, Tyler started to cry. Sharing in our joy the 40 or so other people in the café took to clapping even louder.

*   *   *

Normally marriage preparations take a lengthy amount of time, in most cases six to nine months. Tyler and I wished to become husband and wife much sooner than later. Since both of us would be teaching come 5 September, we chose the 23rd of August to be our wedding date. That happened to be the Feast day for St. Rose of Lima, the first saint of the Americas. St. Rose was renowned for her beauty, her love for the poor, a humble life of penance and mystical prayer.

I had believed God had taken an active role in our budding romance. After our engagement, I came to believe that was definitely the case with our actual commitment. My friend back in California, Father Jerry O'Mahony, Commander, USN, did a great job for us in taking care of all the church details and putting all the necessary paperwork together. He also led our mandatory pre-marriage instructions and, on his own dime, flew to San Antonio, twice for formal marriage instruction and then to officiate at the wedding.

At the beginning of His public ministry, the Lord performed His first miracle by changing water into wine at a wedding. The Church has always seen deep meaning in that first miracle, seeing it as a way God confirmed "the goodness of marriage." And, in line with the teaching of the Holy Father, Pope Paul VI, Tyler and I understood that our "vocation of marriage" would not only be a special reflection of the Lord's presence in the love we shared as husband and wife, it would also be a visible sign to the world of God's continued presence in the Church.

Tyler and I took seriously the responsibility we would have as a married couple to be a visible sign to others of the holiness and sweetness of the love God has for everyone. And like most Christian couples, we looked forward to helping further the aims of the Kingdom of God through "the procreation and education of offspring."

Often, I had thought the issue of intimacy would cause me great embarrassment. But when we had to broach the subject with Father Jerry, I wasn't embarrassed at all. On the one hand the world tells us that a man is not much of a man unless he gets around a lot. On the other hand, chaste living pleases God and the virtue of temperance is not a statement on one's lack of manliness. It is, in the grandest sense an affirmation of one's love of God.

I think the revelation that I was not that experienced in the wiles of the world came as a pleasant surprise to Tyler. I recall how she had so warmly reached out and took my hand and firmly squeezed it, how she had smiled so lovingly. All of us were chosen by God before the creation of the world to be holy and blameless in His sight. I was thankful I had been blessed with the grace to live a life that pleased God. I was grateful that I had been blessed to be in a state of grace for Tyler.

That Tyler had never been with a man before was not a surprise but her admission made my heart soar. I recalled how Tyler had said she wanted God and her parents to be proud of her, how could they not be? I recalled how I had thought she was "something else" and "a real spiritual powerhouse." She really was. With the scent of fragrant vanilla spice in the air, Tyler was truly, as Scripture puts it, "a fragrant offering pleasing and acceptable to God." It was my turn to take her hand into mine and hold tightly.

*   *   *

Tyler and I were married in a simple wedding Mass at 1000, Wednesday, the 23rd of August, 1967 in the base chapel on Randolph AFB, Texas. Father Jerry O'Mahony, Commander, USN officiated. In attendance were Aunt Ruth and a score of Tyler's local and home town friends. Travis had gotten special permission to fly down from the USAFA Prep School. Hitch and his wife, Tiffany, were there too. Little five-year old Emily Reid was our flower girl. Mike Reid was Best Man. His wife Carmen was the Bride's Maid.

Tyler wore her white summer dress and her white turquoise studded western boots. Her long red hair was tied back by a large, cute white bow. As always, she looked beyond amazing. I wore my Marine Corps Dress Blues.

Our Gospel Reading, Tyler and I had chosen from St. Mark.

"At the beginning of Creation, God made them male and female. 'For this reason, a man shall leave his father and mother', and the two shall become as one. They are no longer two, but one flesh. Therefore, let no man separate what God has joined together."

Travis had his friends from the Randolph AFB Honor Guard make a six-man ceremonial sword arch. As we walked under and through it on our way out of the chapel, Tyler kept repeating, "This is so cool. This is so cool."

*   *   *

As we drove the 140 miles from San Antonio to Corpus Christi, Tyler started to hum the song I had written and sang as a proposal. "You write that all by yourself?" she asked.

"Sure did."

"Tune too."

"Yep."

"Not bad. When did you write it?" Tyler asked.

I took my eyes off the road just long enough to give her a quick glance. "Truth be told I wrote it a long, long time ago."

"You ever sing it for anyone else?" Tyler's facial expression transitioned into the cute little pout that I had thought was so syrupy adorable.

"No Mem. I may have come up with the song years ago, but it was written with just you in mind, the young lady I've been looking for all my life."

Tyler's face lit up and she started humming the tune again, all the while holding her left hand out in front of her, wiggling her ring finger, grinning at the little wedding band that had an even littler diamond inlaid in turquoise. Beaming the brightest smile, Tyler turned to me, "Mrs. Tyler Rose Taylor, has a nice poetic ring to it, don't you think?"

Taking my eyes off the road again just long enough to look at Tyler and take it all in, I answered, "a very pleasant poetic ring."

*   *   *

Tyler and I had chosen Corpus Christi for our brief honeymoon because we both had had some good times there when we were younger. Turned out we may have in fact "met" there once before.

During the summer break before her freshman year in college, Tyler and her friends used to head down on the weekends to lay on the beach to sun bathe. She recalled an incident when some six or seven Marine amphibious vehicles came out of the surf literally right on top of them as they were all scantily clad on beach towels.

The time frame she spoke of would have been around the summer of 1963 when I was still active with Company B. That summer we had had a problem of sorts while practicing amphibious operations. The wind had gotten bad and churned up the waves. We got blown way off course when our "amtracks" tried to line up for the landing assault. After landing in the wrong spot, I remembered hitting the beach with my squad and having to set up a skirmish line in the sight of tantalizing sun-bathing beauties.

Have you ever thought about how hard it is to herd cats? That's how hard it is to get Marines to stick to the program when there are pretty women around. The memory made me laugh out loud. Then I imagined in my memory that I may have seen a particularly stunning redhead in a pink bikini. "Tyler," I asked, "you recall if you wore a pink bikini that day?"

"Sure did, it's the only bikini I have. I like to wear it because I get the most sun that way." Tyler's answer had been given in such a matter-of-fact fashion, it seemed funny to me. Then she added, "And I brought it with me."

"You don't say," I said as I looked over at her, smiling.

Tyler grinned back at me.

*   *   *

Intimacy is a precious and beautiful gift from God. That "two shall become as one," how could it not be seen as anything but a gift from our Heavenly Father? About our first days, and nights as husband and wife, my constant thought and prayer was of thanksgiving. I thanked God for Tyler. I thanked God we were husband and wife.

About all our days, and nights since, my constant thought and prayer has been the same.

CHAPTER FIVE

"a time to mourn . . ."
Ecclesiastes 3:2

The years went by and we were happy. Tyler and I were profoundly grateful that we had been blessed to walk in the favor of God. We were thankful beyond measure that we had been blessed with a fervency of love and longing for one another that paralleled that of the lovers in the Song of Solomon. Our anniversaries were spent in Texas. We'd visit Aunt Ruth and then Tyler would get what she called, her "solar fix." She enjoyed sunbathing on the beach. I enjoyed seeing her in her bikini. During the school year, we took great pleasure in the church bowling league. In 1976 we took home the couple's championship trophy. Only one thing was missing.

Tyler and I both loved kids and wanted a house full. After two years of trying to start a family we were getting discouraged and decided to have ourselves checked out. Tyler seemed to be okay but I was not. It turned out, as my doctor put it, I had been born with what he called the most severe case of varicocele that he had ever seen. The doctor said the condition made it highly unlikely I'd ever father a child. But he also said there was always the possibility.

For a while I was depressed, especially because I felt like I had let Tyler down. Tyler didn't see it that way. She was so lovingly supportive. "It's just something we have to accept," she said.

Eventually, after prayer and discussion we went through the screening process and got approved and signed up through Catholic Charities to be put on their adoption list. It was at that point that we found out just how many young couples were out there that also wanted little ones. When we found out that we were way down on the list, we both got involved in the local Big Brother/Big Sister program. The program blessed us with meaningful relationships with some very good youngsters and I like to think Tyler and I made a difference in their lives.

*   *   *

Some years later, right before the holidays in late 1977, Tyler and I started to notice her stomach was getting a bit pooched out. She was also having nausea spells in the morning. We both got excited, thinking that after ten years of marriage, we were finally on the way toward starting a family.

We were wrong.

Tyler's primary care doctor ran all the normal tests. She was not pregnant but did have an extremely elevated white blood cell count. Her lymphocyte reading was way above normal and her platelet count was getting down to a critically low level. A computed tomography was scheduled for the next week.

When the doctor got the radiologist's finding, he called us immediately. It seemed that Tyler had an oversized spleen, nearly three times the size of what it should have been. Her spleen should have been about the size of her tiny fist but instead, it was larger than a softball. A referral was sent to a local oncologist's office and a bone marrow biopsy was scheduled.

The results of the biopsy gave us the diagnosis of stage IV splenic marginal zone lymphoma. That had been the very form of lymphatic cancer Tyler's mother had been stricken with back in the 1950s. The oncologist advised we have Tyler's spleen removed while he and his colleagues researched possible chemotherapy treatments. The splenectomy was scheduled.

*　　*　　*

On Tyler's 32nd birthday, Valentine's Day, February 14th, 1978, she and I had planned a quiet romantic evening at home. I had given Tyler a sterling silver turquoise bracelet. She had given me a gold framed photo of she and I walking under the ceremonial sword arch on our wedding day. Under the glass, next to Tyler's image had been placed a small locket of her hair tied with a teeny pink bow. Written across the photo was "yours always!"

Earlier in the afternoon we had gotten a real treat. Tyler's brother, Captain Travis Devine called from Naval Air Station, Keflavik, Iceland. He was enjoying his assignment as the maintenance officer for the small Air Force detachment of F-4E Phantom fighter aircraft. Travis said he was praying for us and he wanted me to know that while I was partial to one particularly gorgeous little Texas red head, he had taken a shine to a particularly beautiful little Icelandic blonde. Her name was Anna and Travis hoped we could all get together sometime in the summer.

For dinner, I had made my version of Tyler's Tex-Mex enchiladas. I had placed sliced olives on top of the cheese in the shape of a heart. Tyler had made her fantastic southern sourdough biscuits. The Yellow rose I had given her that morning was on the dining table in the little crystal vase purchased years before at the BX at MCRD.

Instead of asking me to open the new jar of strawberry jelly, Tyler tried to open it herself. Having difficulty, she attempted to get more leverage on the jar. She pressed it hard against her stomach. As she strained to twist the cap, Tyler dropped to the floor and cried out in pain. Something as innocuous as trying to open a jar of jelly had ruptured her fragile, oversized spleen.

*   *   *

I got Tyler to the hospital as quick as I could. The drive remains a blur in my mind. In Emergency Tyler was quickly assessed and taken into surgery. Three hours later a doctor and hospital chaplain escorted me to a private consultation room. I was told the surgery had not gone well. Tyler had been taken to the intensive care unit. She still had bad internal bleeding, life threatening low blood pressure and was suffering from hemorrhagic shock. Tyler's blood loss was preventing her body from receiving an adequate flow of oxygen. Her kidneys and other organs were shutting down.

When I finally got in to see Tyler, she was asleep. She was ashen faced. A nurse had tied her hair into a bun like Tyler used to do when she was doing chores around the house. Her breathing was labored and irregular. Her pulse rate was very, very low. I had to clinch my teeth to keep my composure. I walked over to the left side of her bed, leaned over and placed a yellow rose in her left hand and put her pink rosary in her right. After pulling over a chair I sat down next to her and took her hand into mine. I was doing ok until Carmen and Mike showed up. After that, I couldn't contain myself. I cried. They both walked over and placed their hands on my shoulders.

Tyler was on oxygen and being given a blood transfusion and administered intravenous sodium chloride to try to boost her blood pressure. It didn't help.

After nearly an hour of praying and crying, crying and praying, Tyler opened her eyes. She turned toward me. As she looked at me with what had always been gemstone like gleaming hazel eyes, I could tell it was nearly all she could do to force a smile. She said twice, in a muted and raspy voice, "I love you. I love you."

I stood up and leaned over. I started to cry worse as I kissed her. "I love you too," I said.

Taking notice of the rose I had given her, Tyler tried to lift it to me. I reached over and took it from her. In her eyes there welled up huge tears that dropped like rain-drops on her pillow. She managed a broader smile and, reminiscent of our farewell some ten years before at the San Antonio airport, Tyler uttered in a barely audible whisper, "don't forget to water the rose." She closed her eyes. She closed her eyes for the last time.

Mike and Carmen lost their composure too.

I cried as I have never cried before. I wept and wept. I had the sense that my tears came from the deepest recess of my soul. I became self-aware that my wailing had an out of this world quality to it, as if God Himself were crying through me too.

CHAPTER SIX

"There are in the end three things that last;
Faith, hope and love,
and the greatest of these is love."
1st *Corinthians 13:13*

Tyler's funeral Mass was held in Yoakum, Texas at St. Joseph Catholic Church. She was laid to rest close to her parents in its nice little church cemetery. Aunt Ruth, to honor the deep love she knew I had for her niece, got the monsignor to approve the addition of a non-liturgical song at the end of the formal mass proceeding. A local performer sang my favorite song, Charley Pride's "Amazing Love." It was sung a cappella and by song's end, there wasn't a dry eye in the church. The refrain brought me to my knees. God Himself knew how un-worthy I felt to be blessed with Tyler's amazing love. Tyler knew each and every rose I had given her spoke to the depth of my feeling for her. Often, we had talked about how we felt like the lovers in the Song of Solomon. Tyler knew I cherished her as much, if not more than the bridegroom in the story cherished his bride.

*　　*　　*

In the days and nights that shortly followed, I did a lot of soul searching and the only answer I could come up with was that there was no answer. Like King Solomon, I had to just accept things. "All things I probed in wisdom, I said, I will acquire wisdom, but it was beyond me. What is far reaching is deep, very deep. Who can find it?"

But the Good Lord was true to His word, "those crushed in spirit, He saves." God stood by me in my time of broken-heartedness and pulled me through my sense of loss and melancholy. Through God's grace I came to accept that there is a season and time for every purpose under Heaven.

> *"There is a time for love.*
> *There is a time for war.*
> *There is a time to dance.*
> *There is a time to mourn."*

So too, counting my blessings assuaged my anguish. Tyler and I believed God had meant for us to be together. God does have a plan for each of us and when I count my blessings, I especially thank Him for directing my footsteps and lighting my way to Tyler.

A whole chain of events had to happen for me to be blessed with Tyler. I had planned to be a career officer in the United States Marine Corps, but I suffered a career hampering injury. Had that not happened, had I not taken an interest in part time journalism, had I not taken the Christian Focus magazine assignment, had I not gone to the Alamo on that Memorial Day, had I not gone to Kress Five and Dime, Tyler and I would never have been husband and wife. Some marriages are made in heaven.

God's presence and His love for us can be encountered in many simple, subtle, sublime and spectacular ways. To me, the most sublime way in which God can be experienced is in the love a husband and wife share. The Church and mystics like St. John of the Cross tell us that the Song of Solomon is an allegory to describe God's all-powerful, all-encompassing love for us, a love that is brighter than the brightest flame and stronger than death. Tyler and I were blessed to experience that love in the love we shared. Through the grace and blessing of Almighty God, we were blessed to live our own version of the Song of Solomon.

*   *   *

To the Lord, one day is as a thousand years, and a thousand years is as one day. In a sense that is how I view our short ten years of marriage. In the limited time we were together, Tyler and I were blessed to make enough memories to last a dozen lifetimes. And the most cherished of all are the memories of the simplest pleasures of being husband and wife, helping Tyler out of her bubble bath and wrapping a warm towel around her, helping her with house chores when she suddenly broke out in song and danced around with the vacuum cleaner singing Tammy Wynette's "Your Good Girl's Gonna Go Bad" and snuggling up with her and her old army blanket close to the fireplace, listening to Patsy Cline records or just the hissing, crackling and popping of the logs on the fire.

I travel to Texas every year. And on our anniversary, the 23rd of August, I place a single yellow rose on Tyler's grave. I drive to San Antonio and stand in the very spot in the Alamo where the Good Lord first brought us together. I go to Austin, to Barton Springs and walk the pathway we took around Zilker Park. All the while my thought and prayer is of thanksgiving. I thank God for blessing me with Tyler and I thank Him for blessing me with the great privilege of being her husband.

Someday my earthly remains will rest beside Tyler's. That will not be the end of our story. I believe in God. I believe in the resurrection of the body and life ever-lasting. In the land that knows no parting, angels will look on admiringly at two blessed souls lovingly walking hand in hand, my yellow rose of Texas and me.

Profit donated to the Alaskan Shepherd Fund, Catholic Bishop of Northern Alaska and The Leukemia and Lymphoma Society, Rocky Mountain Region.

Rick Miller is a veteran of over 24 years of military service. He lives in Colorado and is an adventure motorcyclist and fisherman.

Made in the USA
Monee, IL
16 May 2024

58371873R00049